Traveling with A Purpose

Published by:

Carol Keller

CarolKeller777@yahoo.com

Copyright 2018

First Printing, 2019

Printed in the United States of America

ISBN: 9781723563874

D1617501

Contents

My Mission Trips

Mexico (1990)
Youth for Christ — taught Vacation Bible School in Mexicali

Russia (1997)
HCJB helping families start up small family businesses and working with Churches Uniting in Global Mission and Russian Farm Community Project

Poland (1998)
Cedar Grove Community Church, Livermore, CA Helped build a church in Warsaw with Greater Europe Mission organization. Learned how to use a jackhammer!

Ecuador (1998)
Visited and served at hospitals singing to patients and sharing the gospel, and visited orphanages in Quito

Greece/Turkey (1998)
HCJB delivered radio equipment to radio stations, and worked with prayer walking ministry

India (1998)
Family Radio — helped distribute 200,000 gospel tracts in Karnal, Ambala, and Chandigarh in the State of Haryana

India (1999)
"Faith" with a capital "F"

Australia/New Zealand (2000)
HCJB World Radio (Heralding Christ Jesus' Blessings) Worked with radio ministry; prayer walks through cities.

California (2001)
Faith Presbyterian Church — helped build homes for and with farm laborers in Visalia through Self Help Organization

Ireland (2001)
Cedar Grove Community Church, Livermore, CA Construction work at Drewstown House Christian Conference Center in Navan, Ireland

China/Hong Kong (2002)
HCJB visited various radio ministry stations

Czech Republic (2004)
Capital Christian Center
Construction work on Teen Challenge Center in Sluknov

Siberia (2004)
International School Project - worked with school teachers, using translators, on how to read and study the Bible and how to teach their students the Bible in the city of Blagoveshchensk

South Africa (2005)
Group originated by Bruce Wilkenson, author of the book *The Prayer of Jabez*, working alongside village people helping them plant vegetable gardens in Swaziland (350 volunteers)

Tanzania (2001, 2004, 2006, 2008, 2009)
Visited daughter, Kathy, missionary in Dar es Salaam—working alongside her in her ministry.

France (2016, 2017)
Working with Kathy in her ministry in Paris.

Japan (2017)
Trip to Tokyo, Hakone, Kanazawa, Kyoto, and Hiroshima.

Paris via Uber (2017)
Trip to BIOLA University, California; and Paris.

Here is a more recent photo of those little boys with their dad, Shawn, and special little sister.
Derrick, Kaleigh, Dad, Jonathan

About this Book

After the passing of my husband at the age of 50, I seemed to be living in a fog. I thought to myself, "Who am I now if I'm no longer John's wife? What do I do now?" Depression set in, life seemed so unbearable, and I was so unhappy. I was working as a Supervisor over secretaries in the Criminal Section of the Attorney General's Office in Sacramento, California.

As time went on, I began sensing God was telling me to retire early and go on mission trips around the world. As I talked with friends about this, a few of them would say, "You can't retire this young! How long can you live without your income?" Becoming very confused, I decided to stop listening to friends and listen to the Lord.

Driving back to my office from lunch one day I prayed, "Dear God, I know you want me to retire and go on mission trips, and I know you will take care of me, but could you please give me a little sign that I am doing the right thing?" Arriving at work I entered my office and there in the middle of my desk was a note from one of the attorneys I worked with which read, "Please see me about retirement." I had chills as I read the note. I grabbed the note and ran into his office saying, "Do you know you are an answer to prayer?" Of course, you don't normally think of an attorney as being an answer to prayer.

I explained what just happened, and he told me he had heard from one of the other attorneys that I wanted to find out how to get information concerning retirement with the State. Then, with a chuckle he replied, "If this doesn't work out for you, I'm going to feel a little responsible."

I am grateful God had the attorney place that note on my desk. It helped bring me into an adventure that I only dreamed about. **So,** before we begin my journey, I would like to pause and share with you "My Testimony –The Moment That Changed My Life". After reading my testimony, let the travels begin!

My Testimony

Many years ago, on Layperson Sunday at my church, I was asked to give my testimony, my son was asked to give his testimony, my daughter was asked to sing a solo, and my husband worked in the sound booth. We were introduced as the "Von Keller Family".

The Moment That Changed My Life

The Bible says in Philippians chapter 1 verse 21: "For to me to live is Christ..."

As I look back on my childhood, I can look back with the understanding that we are products of our parents, they are products of their parents, and, hopefully, with each new generation we learn to become better at parenting. I realize that my parents did the best they were capable of doing in raising us.

But as a little girl, when trying to understand love, I asked my mother, "Why don't you hug me and kiss me anymore?" She replied, "Oh, I did that when you were a baby." So in my childlike understanding, I concluded that only babies were loved and only babies were worthy of love. Not too many years ago, my mother confided in me and said, "I guess I just had too many of my own problems to have any time for you children."

My father, on the other hand, was determined never to physically and brutally beat us as his father did to him. So, instead, he verbally and emotionally beat us, and abused us in other ways, to the point where we considered ourselves completely worthless.

By the age of 16, I felt I had no reason to live. I was fearful of everything, I felt completely worthless, and I didn't want to live. Growing up, I felt as if I were living in a vacuum.

My two brothers and I were born in Scranton, Pennsylvania. Our family moved to Sacramento, California when I was five. During my years in high school, a Christian girl befriended me and began praying for me. She was a faithful friend, always there when I needed her. She was there at my side in the hospital where I lay with a broken back. She was very special, and I remember appreciating her so much, but I also remember not wanting to become like her because she was "too religious."

However, she was successful in encouraging me to attend a Billy Graham crusade during the summer of 1959. I asked my parents if they would take me, and together we sat high in the bleachers. As Billy Graham talked of the love of God and how we were created to have communion with God, he gave an invitation to accept Jesus Christ as personal Lord and Savior. When he gave the invitation to publicly come forward, I felt as if a magnet were pulling at me. I wanted so much to go forward. I knew I had to make this decision on my own, so I told my parents that I wanted to go and sit on the lawn near the stage.

As I walked toward the platform, tears streaming down my face, I stopped, fearful of taking another step. I noticed a family nearby, sitting on the lawn. The husband came toward me and asked if I would like to go forward. I said yes, and with a gentle hand on my shoulder he helped me take that step. I asked forgiveness for my sins and asked Jesus Christ to come into my life to be Lord and Savior.

It was wonderful. Finally, I found someone who loved me. Someone who accepted me just the way I was. I now had a Heavenly Father who would love me and care for me. It was like being blind all my life, and for the first time I was able to see the beauty of a sunrise. I truly went from darkness unto light. I felt an unbelievable weight lifted from me.

The conversion was like a miracle. I wanted to study the Bible and pray about everything. The church I was raised in was very liberal, so I felt it necessary to find one that was Bible-centered. I began attending a Bible church with a passion to learn as much as I could about the Bible.

My conversion caused a complete change in my outlook on life. But the years that followed were not always easy. When you live for years believing one way, it often takes many, many years to change those beliefs and habits of living. There were times when I would put my Bible away and tell God, "I don't need you." But he never let me stray so far that I couldn't come back.

There were many, many changes in my thinking that had to be done. It took months of counseling by a pastor to let myself feel good about me, to tell myself that perhaps, just maybe, there is something good about me. Maybe I'm not the horrible person I always felt I was. And so I was on my way through the very slow process of self-acceptance. But there were fears that I still had to deal with, and one of those fears was marriage.

There was no way that I ever wanted to get married, because of what I saw in my family. If my father were an example of what a husband would be, then I wanted nothing to do with marriage. The pastor helped me see that a man and a woman can love each other and live together happily. It was also helpful for me to see the girlfriend who prayed for me in high school. She married a Christian man and I watched them relate to each other. I saw nothing but love and respect for each other, and a deep love for the Lord who was kept at the center of their marriage.

As I felt better about the possibility of getting married, I thought about how, at a very early age, the Lord had put a love in my heart for Korean children. So, my first desire, then, was to someday marry, give birth to a baby girl, and adopt a Korean child. If I were not to marry, I wanted to go to Korea to work in a Korean orphanage. Well, the Lord gives us the desires of our hearts.

For me, one of those desires is being blessed with a Christian husband, John, who is unbelievably patient. When we were married, I brought to our marriage a little girl inside of me who had not received nurturing—a little girl who never learned to relate to people.

Therefore, the first few years of our marriage were disaster for John. I assumed he would be a husband like my father had been and treated him accordingly. I accused him of everything, I found fault with everything he did, and I tried to mold him into the person I thought he should be. I was hurting our marriage and destroying our relationship. When I finally could see what I was doing, I decided I had to change. With the help of God, studying and memorizing Bible verses, I set out to change my behavior. When I became "livable," I asked John why he put up with me so long because if it were me, I would have left long ago. His reply was, "When I married, it was forever."

John still has to put up with me as I occasionally regress back to those early beginnings, but together we work through my insecurities. He is a man who gives much, much more than he receives. I sent a simple little card to his office one day, and the very next day I received a beautiful bouquet of red roses with a note saying, "Thanks for the card."

I have also been blessed with a Christian daughter, Kathy, who is beautiful on the inside as well as the outside. Whether you are an adult, a teenager, or a child, when you talk with Kathy there will be no doubt in your mind who she believes in, and what she believes. She has a beautiful testimony to all who will listen. At the very tender age of three, she would walk up to an adult and ask, "Do you love Jesus?"

There have been many times when I would learn from her, and I'd think to myself, "I'm the mother, I'm supposed to be teaching her." The Lord has gifted Kathy with a beautiful singing voice, and when she sings, she wants so much for you to feel the presence of the Lord and not have your attention drawn to her. Because of her faithfulness and dedication to the Lord, I know He has something very special for her.

And finally, I have been blessed with a Christian son, Shawn. When Shawn came to us from Seoul, Korea, at age four, we gave him the name "Shawn" because it means "gift from God." He spoke only the Korean language, and he came to us with many, many hurts to overcome, both physical and emotional--hurts that you and I would never have to deal with. But he is a survivor, and he is determined to overcome, and be the best he can be.

In the early years when we were struggling to help him overcome his hurts, I would feel completely helpless—not knowing what to do or say. One day in frustration I asked John, "Why did God send us this child?" and John replied, "because he is going to turn out to be a fantastic adult?" And with the Lord's guidance, that is just what he is in the process of becoming.

Besides John, Kathy, and Shawn, I have been blessed with a church family. I am grateful to all of the people there because I know that I can come to anyone of them in a time of need and they will help me, love me, and accept me just as I am. They are the family I never had.

Obviously, since that moment that changed my life, I have learned more about love and giving. There are two lessons that particularly stand out in my mind that I would like to share with you.

First, when the Lord brings someone to your mind and says, call that person, write that person a note--do it as soon as possible so you won't forget. In that same way, when the Lord puts children in your path, hug those children and let them know they are special and worthy of love. The Lord nudges us for a reason. Someone is in need, and He wants you to help fill that need.

As I seek the Lord's direction in my life, I am reminded of that day when the Lord spoke through Billy Graham to bring me to Him. I am so very grateful, for now I say "For to me to live is Christ . . ."

Leaving My Comfort Zone to Serve God

Many of you have asked me to tell you about my missionary trips. I have returned from India and if I were to give a title to my experiences there, it would be "Leaving My Comfort Zone to Serve God."

As I sat in the San Francisco Airport Monday morning, January 19, 1998, I had no idea what all would take place in the two weeks to come. Why did God want me to go to India? Waiting for the plane, I finally had an opportunity to read the detailed information about the mission trip to India. This trip consisted of 11 men and three women from all over the United States including a man originally from India, but now residing in California who came as our guide and interpreter. We were to distribute 200,000 Gospel tracts to the people of Karnal, Ambala, and Chandigarh in the State of Haryana. There are over 1,000 languages and dialects in India, and the tracts we were to distribute were in the Hindi, Punjabi, Urdo, and English languages.

As I thought about this new experience for me, distributing tracts, I wondered how receptive the people of India would be, and how effective this mission would be. Then I remembered that I brought a book with me that my daughter, Kathy, had given me for Christmas. It is called Hudson Taylor and is the autobiography of a man who brought the gospel to China in the 1800's, and whose influence in China is still felt today. As I began reading this book, there on page 10 Hudson Taylor told of how reading a tract influenced him to know Jesus. I concluded that we were "to plant the seeds" and God would bring in the harvest—this was clearly one of the reasons for my trip to India.

The flight from San Francisco to Hong Kong was 15 hours, and the flight from Hong Kong to India was six and a half hours, arriving in New Delhi, Wednesday, 1:00 AM. From there we took a three-and-a-half-hour bus ride north to the Jewel's Hotel in Karnal. As we entered the hotel lobby, there was an unbelievably potent odor that caused difficulty breathing. One of the ladies (her sixth trip to India) said that it was just cockroach spray! When she saw my eyes nearly pop out of their sockets after discovering we would be sharing our rooms with cockroaches, she said, "No problem, leave the light on at night in the bathroom and you won't step on them—they don't like lights!" Our group, however, decided not to have our rooms sprayed each day—we would rather live with the crawly creatures than inhale the fumes of the poison.

The first day we passed out tracts (we always teamed up with two, three, or four members of the group), swarms of people would surround us asking questions. We were welcomed in the schools and allowed to distribute tracts to the students. They usually asked for English since it is their second language. In every school, the students wore uniforms and were impressively well behaved.

Two of our team members, however, were approached by a very unhappy man who threatened them stating they would have to leave the city or come to the city's security building the next day at 12:30 PM with their passports. The next day the rest of us stayed in the hotel until we heard the outcome of the meeting. The security building consisted of the chief of police and his officers, a room full of advocates (their term for lawyers), and a jail. After the team members explained

17

our purpose, the chief of police and his officers said we were very welcome in their city and asked if they could have tracts for all their family members! As the two team members were leaving, to the advocates they commented, "Jesus is our advocate."

Transportation around the city was on a tricycle rickshaw. It was the ride of a lifetime! We shared the streets with pedestrians, bicyclists, motor bikes, cars, trucks, cows, bulls, pigs, dogs, etc. There were no traffic signs, traffic lights, speed limits, or traffic tickets. There were two lanes of traffic, but the drivers could pretty much choose which lane to ride in—left or right--no matter which direction they were going. Everyone traveled at a fast pace, and there was constant horn honking, but with a smile. No anger. We could have use of a rickshaw and driver for three hours at the price of $1.25.

In Karnal, we had an opportunity to go to a Sikh Temple (reformed Hindu religion). An elderly man was there with his grandson teaching him. Before entering the temple, he explained to us that we had to take our shoes off, wash our hands, and the women had to cover their heads. As we entered, he told us about the holy books on the altar and showed us the bedroom in which the holy books are placed at night. They are put in a bed, covered with a cloth, and the door is locked until the next morning. The Sikh men grow beards, never cut their hair out of respect for God's creation and cover their hair with a turban. A Sikh friend of mine told me they wear a "Kara" which is a steel or iron bracelet to keep them from doing bad things.

Our next stop was Ambala approximately an hour's drive north of Karnal. The address of the hotel was very interesting: "Hotel Batra Palace, Near Bus Stand, Ambala Cantt." We stopped the bus before arriving at the hotel to pass out tracts. By the time I had caught up with my assigned team members, they had already crossed the street and there was no way I could get across to catch up to them. So I decided to return to the bus. As I turned around, coming toward me was a humongous bull on my right and a huge cow on my left. (We had to be very careful because the bulls and cows thought we were handing out food and they would come toward us not too happy to discover that we were not supplying lunch!) I decided to go alongside the cow, the lesser of the two evils—those horns looked mighty scary on that bull.

With my heart pounding like crazy, I finally arrived at the bus and startled the non-English speaking driver who was inside heading toward the back of the bus. When he saw me (I believe he was planning on taking a nap), he became angry, got out of the bus and slammed the door. As I stood there shocked, a group of men were surrounding me, probably trying to figure out what this pale skinned creature was doing in their city. Unable to open the door to the bus, I began to panic. Finally, a man from the group came up and opened the door for me. As I sat in the bus it seemed like forever—waiting for the rest of my team members, the group of men outside stood there the entire time curiously peering into the bus until we left.

When we arrived at the hotel, my roommate, in tears, told me of her frightening experiences that day too. Fear began to overcome us as we thought of all the possible things that could happen to us, both real and imagined. We talked about how during the first few days in India, one of the men in our group became so ill that he had to return to the United States. I recalled the last thing my son, Shawn, had said to me before I left, "Be careful, Mom, be careful." We were told that people were praying for the group in India because "they are putting their lives on the line".

19

We recalled reading about a tour group from the U.S. traveling in another country being attacked.

That Sunday afternoon I learned a new term I had not heard before. The lady I roomed with said it is "gallows humor." Webster's Dictionary defines it as "humor that makes fun of a very serious or terrifying situation." We were so terrified that we locked our hotel door and spent the afternoon talking, crying, and laughing hysterically. We planned how we would put the bed against the door and hide in our portable clothes closet. We talked about how we could be put in jail and mistreated. Perhaps the Peace Corps would come save us. It felt healthy to laugh so much, releasing our tension. We figured, however, by morning our hair would have fallen out because of all the stress we were going through. By morning I had become ill with a very upset stomach. It was a comfort to me because I felt it would be so easy to die of illness and so difficult to be sent to prison! We both definitely felt like we flunked "Missionary".

Needless to say, we did go out again to pass out tracts. We found we had nothing in which to be afraid. We turned our fear into a wonderful love for these gracious people. We found them to be curious toward us, and not in any way threatening. In fact, the closer we came to having to leave India, the sadder we became. On the day we had to depart, many tears were shed by my roommate and me.

Living conditions are very difficult for many people in India. In Karnal and Ambala we saw people living in torn tents along the side of the streets. Others only had blankets. Public bathrooms are a rarity. In the city of Ambala, every so often the entire city would lose its electricity. Each hotel room had one battery-operated light just for those occasions. Every morning we were awakened to what sounded to be like an air-raid siren. I believe it was to replace the rooster—at least it was that early in the morning! It was interesting to discover the milk we drank was from buffaloes (very delicious, I might add). We were told they can get much more milk from a buffalo than from a cow. Most of the food was very spicy; with few meat dishes since most Indian people are vegetarians. The sacred cows roamed the streets confident they would not become someone's prime rib dinner.

In Ambala, I met a wonderful Christian family who invited me to their home on several occasions. Geetanjli James, the 29-year-old daughter of this family, became a wonderful friend. Although the family had very few material possessions, they were so very generous. Each time I visited, Geetanjli would try to find some little gift to give me—one of her books, a small calendar, or a bookmark. The family loved to listen to Gospel music and messages on cassette tapes, but their tape recorder was broken. I was able to purchase a cassette tape recorder/radio at the hotel for them and they were so thankful. It was touching to hear them pray and thank Jesus for the gift.

I recall one night in my hotel room talking to God saying it would be so nice to take home one of the "suits" the women wear in India. A suit consists of a dress, long pants, and a shawl to wear over the shoulders. But I remembered I promised God when I went on a mission trip, I was not there to shop for myself. (I decided if I saw something for Kathy or Shawn, I would purchase it, but that was all.) So, I put the thought of a suit out of my mind.

The next day I had been invited by Geetanjli to have lunch at her home. As we sat on the sofa and talked, she said, "I asked Jesus what I should give my friend Carol for a gift, and He told me a suit". I could hardly believe what I was hearing! She told me she had a suit that she had not yet worn and wanted me to have it. My first thought was that it was too much for her to give me since her family had so little. Then I thought about how she came up to my shoulder and it would never fit. She asked me to try it on and as I did, I told her, "I guess Jesus stretched it out because it fits!" She also gave me a beautiful piece of pink silk material to have a suit made for Kathy when I returned home. As we enjoyed that time together, I thought about the Bible verse Psalm chapter 37 verse 4, "Delight thyself also in the Lord; and He shall give thee the desires of thine heart." I always thought that verse meant only things we prayed and asked for how wrong I was.

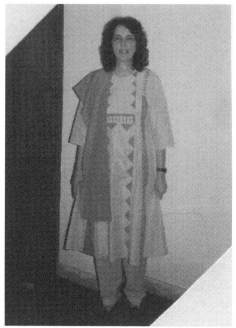

Gift from Geetanjli

After two weeks of an amazing experience in India, we said our tearful goodbyes and headed for home. Upon arriving in San Francisco, I purchased a Greyhound bus ticket to

Sacramento. There at the bus depot was a Sikh waiting in line. I told him I just returned from India and loved the country and the people. We sat together on the bus and he told me he is living with relatives and has been in America for four months. He said he would like to learn English better. I offered to help him in any way I could, excited to be able to continue my mission to Indian people right here at home in Sacramento.

I found the people of India to be the most gracious, loving, and kind people I have ever met. More than once we heard, "If you are happy, than I am happy". When asked if I would go back to India, my reply is: "Yes, in a heartbeat!"

I have learned so much on this trip to India it is just the beginning of what is out there for me, and what God has for me to do for Him.

Geetanjli's family

A Mother Theresa orphanage

Happy school children

"Faith" with a Capital "F"

Can you imagine my surprise when my Sikh friends, originally from India, now living in Sacramento, invited me to a wedding in the city of Karnal—the very city I went to on a mission trip a year ago! In fact, it is the city in which a pastor and his church have been praying for me to return. I believe the Lord was nudging me, just a little, telling me I should return.

Since my retirement, I have had many opportunities to serve the Lord, but my heart is with the people of India and this is what I must write about. "Faith" with a capital F comes to mind as I think back on this marvelous experience.

Faith: Before the Trip
"...but you go and proclaim the Kingdom of God..."
Luke 9:60

I met Pastor Morris P Lal, his wife Sosan, and children Mercy (10), Mayank (6), and Karishma (Dolly) (3) in the streets of Karnal while on a mission trip with a Christian radio ministry in January of 1998. Pastor Morris' church is called the House of Prayer and meets in his home. As we wrote letters back and forth, I learned of the increase of persecution of Christians in India. I had attended a prayer vigil earlier this year of many Indian churches in the Bay area, and had a petition signed by Christians in Sacramento, both church members and Bible study members. The petition was addressed to the President of India asking to intervene in the persecutions of the Christians. I felt God speaking to my heart to go back to India to give encouragement to Christians and let them know of the many people in America praying for them.

Pastor Morris' family

26

Knowing, without a doubt, that going back to India was Gods will for my life, everything would go smoothly, right? Wrong! Since I would be going by myself, there were many things I would have to work out which normally would be taken care of by a tour director. Here are a few obstacles that tested my "Faith:"

- Four days before leaving, I had not yet received confirmation of my return flight out of New Delhi, India. That afternoon, I attended a Bible study asking for prayer for confirmation of that flight. When I returned home, I received a call that I would have a flight home.
- Neither the pastor's family nor the Sikh family has a telephone. Consequently, trying to communicate with them was a challenge. They would call me on a public phone, leave a number, and I would call back hoping to get a line clear enough to communicate. Three days before I left for India, I finally reached Pastor Morris and he confirmed that he and his family would be at the airport to pick me up (a two and a half-hour drive from his home).

- Two days before I left for India, I literally YELLED over the phone to my Sikh friends telling them that I would be at the Jewel's Hotel on Wednesday, March 3, hoping they had heard me (and hoping my neighbors didn't!).

- Finally, I felt all was well and I could begin thinking about what to pack. But then, again on the second day before I was to leave, I received a call from my brother that our mother (who was 92 years old and had recently come down with the flu) had died. After hanging up the phone, I prayed to God asking what I should do. As I opened my Bible, I read in Luke chapter 9 verses 59 and 60: "He said to another man, 'Follow me'. But the man replied, 'Lord, first let me go and bury my father.' Jesus said to him, 'Let the dead bury their own dead, but you go and proclaim the kingdom of God.'" I had complete peace about going to India, and after talking with my two brothers, I then took care of the arrangements to have a graveside service for our mother upon my return.

The next day, as I began packing my clothes, some dried fruit, crackers, etc., I packed my usual two pens. But the thought kept going through my mind—take three pens. So I decided to pack an extra pen. Then, the thought came to pack a flashlight—but why—I would be staying at the hotel and there would be no need for one—I packed a flashlight anyway.

Faith: The Day of the Trip
"...the Lord your God will be with you..."
Joshua 1:9

As I awoke early March 1, 1999, I awoke terrified, fearful of what I was about to do. I would be traveling alone to a foreign country, not knowing what to expect, and up until the last few days everything seemed so uncertain. I thought about all the people who said they would be praying for me, but still I was experiencing fear. Looking in the back of my Bible, I had written down verses on various topics. One verse was concerning Job's highest and greatest expression of faith. That's what I needed to read about, I thought.

However, instead of turning to the verse in Job, my eyes had caught the verse directly below, which was Joshua chapter 1 verse 9. As I turned to it, I began reading, "Have I not commanded you? Be strong and courageous. Do not be terrified; do not be discouraged, for the Lord your God will be with you wherever you go." A "peace that passes all understanding" came upon me as I thanked God for this opportunity to serve him, without fear, and with complete faith in Him. I set out for India with a heart filled with faith.

During the flight to Los Angeles, I talked with a couple about my plans. As we talked, I told them of my concern that I had a short time to locate Malaysia Airlines, would be staying overnight in Malaysia en route to India, and had no guide to hold my hand. As I finally located the shuttle bus pick-up spot, I noticed the couple from the flight was there. They looked at me, smiled from ear to ear, and pointed to a man carrying a huge backpack standing a close distance from them. Immediately, I walked over to him, and he told me his name was Tim.

29

He said he was from Kentucky, was going on a mission trip to India on Malaysia Airlines. He said he usually goes with a group but this was his first time going alone. The Lord provided me with a guide to India. Later, as Tim and I sat talking, waiting for our flight, he mentioned that the only thing he forgot to bring with him was a pen! I said I just happen to have an extra one!

On the flight to India I prayed that Pastor Morris and his family would not get their feelings hurt when I told them I would be staying at the Jewel's Hotel in Karnal, and not in their home. The hotel would have bathroom facilities we are accustomed to. Remembering that on my two previous trips I became very ill from the spicy Indian food, it was comforting to know that the hotel restaurant would have a large variety of foods in which to choose. However, I had no idea how deeply this precious family was going to touch my heart.

Faith: The Time in India

"...all these things will be added to you."
Matthew 6:33

D uring the drive from the airport to Karnal, Pastor Morris asked me to be very careful how I spoke. Because of much persecution going on, he asked me not to use words like "mission" or "missionary." Since foreigners are assumed to be Christians, he asked that I wear the Indian dress so that I would not stand out quite as much.

I cannot say enough about the generosity of the people of India, Pastor Morris stopped by their home before taking me to the Jewel's Hotel. As we entered, they told me they had taken a loan from friends and relatives and fixed up a small room for me to sleep in and constructed a "Western" bathroom—a bathroom with a toilet! Indian bathrooms consist of a hole in the floor. Above the bed on a shelf was a picture of me showing me this was to be my room.

They were the only rooms in their home that were painted (a pretty light blue) and that had tile floors. The other rooms were dirt floors, and their bedroom floor was made of loose bricks.

I thought, O.K. Lord, I guess I'll be staying with them. As I looked at the sagging springs on the bed, I thought if the pain in my back becomes unbearable (due to a broken back several years ago and ever since then in need of a very firm mattress), then I will just lay on the floor at night. Then I looked up and saw mosquitoes dive bombing through the windows that were without screens or glass. My first thought was "Malaria--Oh, no!" Needless to say, I knew I would be staying with this wonderful family.

The first two nights, however, I did stay at the hotel so that the Sikh family could get in contact with me. Pastor Morris and Sosan visited me the following day at the hotel. As I sat on the bed, they noticed that the mattress was very firm and asked if I like a bed that hard. I told them yes, that it was better for my back. The following day they returned to the hotel to bring me to their home. As I walked into "my room," there was a bed of wood (a cedar chest) with a thin firm mattress. They said they went to the market that morning.

Also, they handed me a small item to plug into the wall socket at night to keep the mosquitoes away—and it worked—not one mosquito had me as a midnight snack.

There, next to the bed, was a small table with foods they knew I could eat that would not bother my stomach-foods such as bananas and oranges (they have peelings, so you do not have to be concerned about them being washed with their water), chips, a loaf of bread, bottled water, etc.

That night I discovered why that still small voice was telling me to bring a flashlight. Every so often the electricity in the entire village would go out for a short time—no problem, the Lord had me come prepared!

After my stay with the pastor's family, I had a wonderful experience staying two nights in the village of the Sikh family and attending the wedding. The wedding lasted two days, the first day a morning tea party, and an evening dinner.

The next morning the wedding ceremony in the temple took place and there was a party in the afternoon. During the temple ceremony, the bride followed the groom as they walked around the altar four times making vows to each other. On the altar was their holy book called the Guru Granth Sahib.

A Sikh Wedding

The families of the bride and groom arranged the marriage. I have never seen so much participation by all families and friends involved.

The father of the groom and the father of the bride placed garlands over their heads giving their blessings to the union and uncles of the bride and. groom did the same.

It is tradition that after the wedding the bride moves into the home of the groom. From grandparents to the smallest child, they are all there supporting and caring for each other. Incidentally, during my stay with the Sikh family, I was able to watch one of the Sikh men put on his turban. I was amazed to discover that the turban material is 21 feet long!

Traditional Sikh turban

As I think back, I smile, remembering the contrast of the two families I lived with. Hindi is the main language spoken in the village of the Pastor. The greeting for non-Christians was "namaste," which means "hello or good-bye". For the Christians the greeting was, "Jai Masihi Ki," which means, "Praise the Lord". There I was called "sister." In the morning I could hear Pastor Morris waking and the first words of out his mouth were, "Thank you Jesus, thank you Jesus".

In the Sikh village, the Punjabi language is spoken. The greeting in the Sikh village was "sat shiri akal." There I was known as "Keller" We slept with open doors and windows and in the morning from 4 AM to 6 AM, over a loud speaker, a man at the Sikh Temple repeated prayers in the Punjabi language--heard by the entire village. Sleep for me was not going to happen. So, there I lay awake in the bedroom with grandma, daughter, grandson, and granddaughter watching another family--a mother bird and her babies. As the sunlight began peeking through the open doors and windows, I lay in bed watching the mother bird fly in and out tenderly feeding her little babies in the nest she had built in the rafter of our bedroom.

India has always been known for its freedom of religion. For many years there have been few reported cases of persecution. However, there is a small group of militant Hindus who proclaimed that they want only Hinduism in India. Just last year there were about 200 cases of persecution—particularly targeting Christians. They have taken young boys out of school to train them to commit violent acts toward the Christians. When I asked why they are not going after the other religious minorities, I was told they had, but "they have swords." In other words, the other religions fight back; they know the Christians will not fight back. Just before I arrived in India, an Australian evangelist and his two sons were burned to death in their car. This family had been working with lepers in a small village. While I was there, one of the pastors was put in jail. When I said to Pastor Morris that it is sad for his family, his response was that it was much safer for him to be in jail. Otherwise he would be killed.

I was able to attend church services indoors, which usually lasted three to three and a half hours. These new Christians hunger to hear the word of God. Sosan and I visited women in their homes, and we went to villages to visit groups encouraging them in their newfound faith. But for the safety of myself, and the safety of the pastor, I did not attend outdoor baptism services, or any other service held out in public viewing.

Pastor Morris' congregation

To protect Pastor Morris and his family, each time a person comes to know the Lord, that person signs a paper giving name, father's name, address, age, and stating that he/she was not converted by force, has not given any money, and has not changed religions--just accepted Jesus Christ into his/her heart. I was told not to write about the blood of Jesus in a letter, mail would be stopped. Many years ago the current Prime Minister said, "Let the Christians sleep and they will go away." Recently, when a young man was showing the "Jesus" film in a local village, he was attacked, and his throat and arm were cut. He was able to escape but because of the shed blood, many villagers became Christians. I believe that Prime Minister knew what the outcome would be as a result of persecution.

The Lord led Pastor Morris to become a pastor. Since he does not work other than pastoring, I asked how he received income since the church members are extremely poor. He replied, "With tears I would pray asking the Lord's guidance, and he would lead people like you to us."

One evening I asked the pastor and his wife, "What are your dreams and goals for the future?" Expecting to hear "a church building," their response was, "We would like to start an orphanage." Amazing—I thought! Their desire is to care for homeless children, and their thinking is that one building could be used for both an orphanage and a church.

One of the Bible study groups I attend in Sacramento collected money as a gift for me to take to India. Upon receipt, Pastor Morris immediately stopped to give thanks to Jesus. The money, I was told, would be used for transportation to other villages to proclaim God's love.

With deep concern for Pastor Morris, his wife, and their children, I asked what they would do if danger came to them. With unwavering faith and complete trust in God, he said, "If the Lord wants us to leave, we will leave; if He wants us to stay, we will stay!"

Faith – After the trip
"...go and make disciples...I will be with you always..."
Matthew 28:19-20

At the baptism services Pastor Morris hires someone to take pictures because purchasing a camera would be too costly. Before leaving India, I bought two rolls of film and left my camera with him. Upon my return, after talking with a friend about all my experiences, I received a package in the mail from her—a new camera! God's continuing provision!

Often, I am asked about my eye condition, macular degeneration. There is a definite change from when I was first diagnosed, but I am doing O.K. When I think about how the Lord takes care of the smallest details of my life, I know, without a doubt, He will take care of my most difficult challenges.

Knowing Pastor Morris as I do and knowing the Lord led me to his ministry, I feel strongly about helping this ministry. He is one of the most dedicated men of God I have ever known. Everyone he speaks to hears about his love for Jesus. Many have asked what can be done. At the present, Pastor Morris has approximately 100 people attending his services, and continually grows. The room in his home bursts at the seams trying to hold that many people. I plan on sending a check to their ministry in the fall, after the heat of their summer returns to bearable living conditions. Have you ever thought to yourself, "I wish I could give more'? This is the perfect opportunity to do so. Every U.S. dollar sent to India is worth 40 Rupees to them. The Lord knows their needs and He will supply.

It was such a tremendous encouragement to know many of you were praying for me while in India. I know, without a doubt, I remained healthy because of it. Thank you for your prayers and for your continuing interest.

Through this experience, my "Faith" has grown tremendously. I could see the joy and happiness shining in the faces of these people as they learn about Jesus and the Bible and learn to put complete trust in Him. God takes care of every detail of our lives. So why do we worry? My prayer is that everyone who reads this will be encouraged to trust God completely.

JAMBO! (Hello) Family and Friends

What a wonderful experience visiting Kathy in Dar es Salaam, Tanzania! Just had to write about it!

IN GOD'S HAND
". . . Is anything too hard for the Lord?"
Genesis 18:14

On December 28, 2000, when I departed from the Sacramento Airport, little did I know that I would be spending over 24 hours in airplanes—some hours on land, but most in the sky! My first destination was St. Paul, Minnesota, and the snowy weather there caused an hour delay out of Sacramento.

When we finally arrived in St. Paul, I literally ran to Gate G8 realizing there was probably no way the plane would still be there. Upon arrival, I was thrilled to see two airline employees at the gate, and I asked, "Were you waiting for me?" One of the employees replied, "No, not really", and then asked, "Are you Carol Keller?" I was soon to learn there had been a problem with the plane, which caused an hour delay. That was the good news. The bad news was that I was told I could not take my carry-on suitcase with me because the plane was full. But I couldn't let them check in my luggage—in it contained bottles of solution for contact lenses and other breakable items for Kathy! I convinced them to let me "take some things" out of my carry-on before boarding the

40

plane. I literally stuffed my coat pockets and stuffed two huge bags, which I put under my coat. It didn't make much sense to give them a practically empty suitcase when most of its contents were under my coat. To my embarrassment, I felt much like a little old bag lady! As I boarded the plane, a lady in front of me took one look at my protruding stomach, sweetly smiled and said, "You go ahead of me." Is it possible she thought I was . . . no, no I am much too old!

Once I was on the plane, the door closed, and we were on our way to have the plane de-iced. As we began to taxi down the runway, the plane stopped, the captain reported there was another problem and we would have to be taxied back for yet another airplane check. By this time, we were wondering if we really should be on this plane! We knew it would probably be two to three hours before take-off. We had the option of exiting the plane to make other arrangements or waiting it out. On an international flight, once you do exit the plane you cannot come back—you don't have the option of getting your hand stamped to come and go as you please! So, there we sat, and all around me were Americans stressing and complaining about what will happen if they miss their next flight. But wouldn't you know it. Sitting right next to me was a couple from India on their way to New Delhi. They were talking, laughing, and thoroughly enjoying their time together.

After a delay which seemed like forever and

another de-icing, we took off for Amsterdam. As I looked at my ticket, I knew there was no way possible that I would arrive in Amsterdam to catch my flight to Kilimanjaro, eventually arriving in Dar es Salaam. How could I get in contact with Kathy to tell her it may be a day or two before I would arrive, if there even were flights that soon? As panic set in, those feelings of fear and worry started surfacing. However, I recalled the Thursday night Bible study I attend. These wonderful friends surrounded me and prayed specifically for safety and timely connection of my flights. As I thought back, it was reinforced to me that prayer is not just a request for answers, but prayer is a blanket that covers us with a peace that reminds us that the **Lord is in control of every situation**—all we need do is trust Him. I sat back in my seat, not knowing what would happen but knowing, without a doubt, that the Lord had everything already worked out.

Upon arrival in Amsterdam, I was informed that my next flight had been delayed for two hours! This gave me just enough time to board my flight to Kilimanjaro and be on my way to my final destination Dar es Salaam. Upon arrival in Dar es Salaam, I discovered that my "almost empty" carry-on arrived, but my two 60-plus pound suitcases did not. Companies that want airlines to ship goods for them will pay the airlines to have passenger luggage bumped. My luggage, probably due to its size, became the "chosen bumped". After filling out the proper luggage forms concerning my delayed bags, I was handed a $50 bill in U.S. currency. Surprised I asked,

"What is this for?" The reply was, "Go buy yourself a toothbrush." I was then told my luggage would be at the airport "tomorrow"—tomorrow, however, in Africa has many meanings. Last year a mother of one of the missionaries sent a package from the U.S. in February—it arrived in August. Much to the surprise of Kathy and me, the luggage arrived the next evening around midnight.

Sights and Sounds of Dar es Salaam

Traveling on the roads from the airport was quite an experience! Kathy simply said, "Just pretend you are on a roller coaster." I would have much rather preferred a Ferris wheel! No wonder before coming to Africa, Kathy said you might want to bring a neck brace.

Arriving at Kathy's home, I met her two roommates Betty and Julie, and the night watchman, Saidi (sa e dee). Saidi watches over their home from 6 PM to 6 AM. Each night several slices of buttered bread and a thermos of hot water for tea are put out on the back porch for a snack for him. For Saidi, this is his livelihood. As we drifted off to sleep, it was such a comfort knowing he was outside keeping us safe from harm.

All year round, windows are left open—a sweater or light jacket is all that is ever needed and that is seldom. Sleep was accomplished with a fan blowing on me all night. With the moonlight shining through the high window, I crawled into bed pulling down my mosquito net and watched as the net danced to the breeze from my fan.

My first night is one I will never forget. I awoke at 4:15 AM to the sound of the Muslim call to prayer blaring over loud speakers at a nearby Mosque. Can you imagine prayers over loud speakers in America? I don't think so. Unable to sleep, I lay in bed waiting for the sun to come up and when it did what an experience! There was such a wonderful variety of birds singing. Sounds filled my room. I felt as if I was in the middle of a jungle, and any moment I would hear Tarzan swing by on a vine calling out his famous "cry of the jungle"!

The sound of giant crows seemed to be in stereo, and the sight of dozens of them was a little eerie to say the least. I learned that Tanzania was overrun with weaverbirds (birds—related to the finch—which build elaborately woven nests in trees). Trees were dying off because of the overabundance of these nests. To solve the problem, crows were brought over. Now they are overrun with crows to the extent that it looks and sounds like Alfred Hitchcock's movie "The Birds".

As I lay in bed, a horrible loud banging sound hit the roof! My first thought was someone threw a bomb or huge rock. In the morning, I was told there is a mango tree next to the house, and every so often a mango drops hitting our tin roof. It was as if a bowling ball were dropping on the floor and rolling down the lane in a bowling alley! The next sound was a door slamming so loud I thought it would break the hinges. I said to myself, "Wow! Someone must really be angry." I was happy to discover it was a beautiful breeze blowing through the house.

"A time to weep . . . A time to mourn . . ."
Ecclesiastes 3:4

When a green tarp is set up at the entrance of a home, it is the sign of death. Just across the street a 35-year-old woman, mother of a 3 year old, died of AIDS. Her husband died a month earlier. We could hear friends and family mourning throughout the first night. The following day, bus (dala dala) after bus would pick up scores of people to drive them to the church for the burial service. The second evening outside our window we heard beautiful hymns being sung until 2 AM. For a month, friends and relatives would come to visit and show their respects to the family. Three days later a green tarp is set up on our street at yet another home—this time the death of a 25-year-old man who died of Malaria. AIDS and Malaria are two of Africa's biggest killers.

We visited Zanzibar, an island a few miles off the coast of Tanzania. Our Christian guide was Ola Ola, fondly called by his friends Ola Ola Coca-Cola. As we became acquainted with him, he described how difficult it is to be a Christian and live in Zanzibar because of discrimination. He asked if we could find a loving couple in America who would adopt his two small children (a boy

45

and a girl) to have the chance at a better life.

In Zanzibar, one of our stops was in Stone Town. We were taken to a dank, cramped, underground prison where people were kept until sold as slaves. It contained a separate prison for men, and one for women and children. There were two cement seating areas in the shape of a "V" and the opening in the middle of the "V" was used as a toilet. The space was so cramped that standing up was impossible. The people were so packed in that men, women, and children often suffocated. My heart was so torn apart by what the guide was telling us that tears filled my eyes. With a puzzling look on his face he said, "But it isn't happening anymore." He didn't understand that just the thought that any human being could be so cruel to another was too unbearable to hear.

CALLED BY GOD

". . . Here am I! Send me." Isaiah 6:8

Kathy has a tremendous heart for the people of Africa. Along with teaching Bible and computer classes at the Haven of Peace Academy, Kathy works as a leader of the junior high and high school youth. She has a ministry with young girls discipling them, works with a church plant, and is involved in other activities including music, and learning the Swahili language.   After spending time in Africa, I discovered that being a missionary means that the list goes on and on.

Just as God's hand was with me on this trip to Tanzania (and every day), His hand is also with Kathy.

Love and blessings,

Mama Kathy (Kathy's mother)

HOME AGAIN

I have been reading the best seller *The Prayer of Jabez* by Bruce Wilkinson. It is a wonderful book, and praying this prayer daily has definitely been a life-changing experience:

"Oh, that You would bless me indeed, and enlarge my territory, that Your hand would be with me, and that You would keep me from evil, that I may not cause pain!" I Chronicles 4:10

There have been many opportunities to serve others—family, friends, fellow workers, elderly people, and families from India now living in Sacramento. In addition, this summer I will have the opportunity to find housing and transportation for an evangelist from India coming to Sacramento. In September, I will help with repairs to a building at a Christian conference center in Navan, Ireland. I am especially excited about the opportunity to be a part of a mission trip with a church group from Faith Presbyterian Church in Sacramento. We will be going to Visalia, California, to help build a home for the family of a farm laborer.

There are many, many people in need. It is my prayer that we will all search for God's will through His Word, and through prayer, that each one of us will be a shining light for those in need.

Tanzania, the Keyboard, and Egypt

Dear Friends and Family, my friend and co-worker, Cindy, told me her husband "expected" to read about my experiences in Tanzania, East Africa. He has read my other letters and said he wanted to hear more. So, Ron, here it is.

Flights and More Flights

I am so thankful to my brother, Bill, for helping me get to the San Francisco Airport with my entire oversized luggage. I couldn't have done it without him. We left Sacramento at 3:30 AM on December 27, 2003. I had a carry-on, a 65+ pound suitcase, and an encased five-foot-long keyboard weighing 90 lbs.! As we entered the airport with my entire luggage, Bill handed me the handle of the keyboard case and rushed outside to park his car. I found the keyboard was so heavy that I couldn't lift it to prop it up against the wall. So, there I stood with this huge case half way off the floor. Two young men came toward me, and I asked if they would help me. One young man asked if it was a guitar, and I said no that it was a keyboard. Their eyes widened as one asked, "WOW, are you in a band?" As I smiled and said no, I was trying to visualize myself in this "Senior Citizen Band"—just couldn't picture it.

Kathy playing the 90 lb. keyboard

The four flights to Tanzania were a total of about 24 hours, plus about 10 hours sitting in the various airports—San Francisco, Washington, Amsterdam, and Kilimanjaro. For traveling, I wore a black and red suit which happened to be the colors of the flight attendants' outfits on the flight to Amsterdam. During that 10-hour flight, I walked to the rear of the plane to stretch my legs and get a drink of water. Since there were no flight attendants present, passengers would approach me asking for water or orange juice, mistaking me for a flight attendant. So being the Biblical Martha that I am, I felt right at home. I had so much fun as I stayed in the rear of the plane serving drinks to the passengers!

Life in Tanzania

Dar es Salaam, Tanzania, East Africa has a population of about three million with 65,000 Gujarati Indians. There are three seasons: hot, hotter, and hottest! December and January are the hottest.

I am so thankful to John, my husband, for taking our family on camping trips when the children were young. I am quite sure that is one of the reasons Kathy does so well as a missionary in Tanzania.

Often the electricity goes off; the phones go out; and the water tank has to be monitored almost daily. A bowl of soapy water is placed in the sink for washing hands throughout the day, thereby saving water. Electricity is purchased at the "Electricity Store". You take what looks like a credit card, purchase so many units of electricity, take it home and insert it into a box on the wall—and Voila—electricity—most of the time. Kathy has neither a washing machine nor dryer, so clothes are washed in a bucket in the bathroom and hung out on a line to dry.

When I left California, I did not have curly hair. Since I did not bring a hair dryer, I stood on a chair to blow dry my hair under the ceiling fan. It didn't take long to discover that trying to style my hair was useless. With 90+ degree heat, and nearly 90% humidity, I would end up with more curls than Shirley Temple did as a little girl!

What's that on the Floor?

It is common to see creatures crawling on the floor. One day we found what looked like a plump, three-inch worm. It turned out to have what seemed like about 40 tiny legs. I had the honor of scooping it up and tossing it outside. Guess that was my initiation for staying at Kathy's new flat. I remembered Kathy once writing, "I love to have geckos. They are a welcome addition to our households cuz they kill the bugs for their lunch. I saw one just yesterday and smiled to myself— thank you for coming by, my little bug-eating friend☺". Since shoes are always removed at the front door, I learned to be careful where I stepped.

One evening as I lay in bed under the window, I heard a "thump" on the windowsill. I sat up and starred eye-to-eye with a fairly good-sized rat. We both froze, and he quickly scampered off, but it took me a while to unfreeze. The windows are always open. I am so thankful Kathy had screens put on the windows before moving in—the rat fell between the open louvered window and the screen; otherwise it may have ended up on my head, and I definitely would have had an unwanted bed partner.

Tanzania Transportation

Kathy's car did not start one morning, and I commented on how well she took things. Her reply was that things happen in threes: electricity went out, phone went out, and now the car has died. Evidently, you just learn to live with all the inconveniences. In order to get your car repaired, you don't look up a local repair shop in the phone book and have your car towed. Kathy asked a taxi driver and another missionary to recommend a mechanic. Once a mechanic is found, he comes to your home, checks out the car and tells you what to purchase. You purchase the part or parts needed, and the mechanic returns to do the installation.

All car owners must have their car insurance document and ownership papers taped to the windshield on the passenger's side of the car. Most police officers are on foot and can stop you at a moment's notice for any reason. Kathy would tell me not to make eye contact with them. However, one day an officer did flag her down. As he looked at Kathy, and then looked at me, he asked, "Are you her mother?" I replied, "Yes". He then said, "I would like your permission to marry her". Kathy and I both smiled, and then were allowed to go on our way. What a country!

It is illegal to make a U-Turn in Dar es Salaam. Sometime ago, Kathy was taking a young girl home and since there are almost no street signs they had trouble finding her street. Kathy did the unthinkable and made a U-Turn. She ended up having to go to the police station where she received a lecture and told she could possibly go to jail. Kathy told the officers that she was very sorry she made a U-Turn and that if she has to go to jail, then she will just have to go to jail. At that point, one of the officers said, "You are forgiven." She was then released to go home. What a country!

Taxis have no meters. It was fun to listen as Kathy would ask a taxi driver what it would cost to travel to a certain destination. He would give his price and every time, in the Swahili language, Kathy would say it was much too high! Back and forth they would argue a price until they finally came to an agreement—sometimes Kathy had the final say, sometimes the taxi driver did. It was interesting to note that taxi drivers usually put in just enough gas to get to their next couple of destinations, seldom more than a quarter tank of gas.

Africans, New Christians, Missionaries

Older women are highly respected in Tanzania. As I traveled throughout Dar es Salaam, many African people would make a point of speaking to me, greeting me with "Mama". They were very, very, friendly.

Kathy and I served an "American" dinner to the Indian ladies and their children. We used some of our favorite family recipes: Aunt Betty's salad (minus the artichoke hearts—couldn't find any in Dar es Salaam); Uncle Rick's creamed corn (minus the Parmesan cheese); Aunt Carol's twice-baked potatoes, and Apricot/Pineapple pastry. As Kathy invited the Indian ladies to dinner, she said BYOC—bring your own Chutney (and/or spices). We thought they might feel our bland food would need some spicing. As the ladies ate, they told us it was their first American food. They enjoyed the dinner, even though it was quite different from what they are accustomed to. The twice-baked potatoes were a favorite.

After shopping for the food, preparing the fruits and vegetables by soaking them in bleach water, and finally serving the meal, I discovered two things. One, because most food is imported, often the cost is about three times more than it would have cost here in America. Two, it takes about three times longer to shop for the food and prepare it. We are so spoiled in America!

If you eat rice, mangos, pineapples, coconuts, tomatoes, and other fruits and vegetables, it is very inexpensive to eat in Tanzania. Mangos cost just pennies. Most all other foods and items are imported; therefore, the cost of living can be extremely high. A very common African dish is rice, potatoes, carrots, chicken, and spices—almost like a stew. I recall one day Kathy asking me how long eggs last in the refrigerator. I asked how the expiration information on the carton was worded—she had a good laugh over that! What carton, what wording? We become so accustomed to the way life is over here. When I arrived home to Sacramento, I couldn't get enough drinks out the faucet since you never drink water there unless it is boiled or bottled water.

It is easy to understand why house workers are needed. Everything is very time-consuming—shopping, cleaning, laundry, and preparing food before cooking, etc. Because of this, almost everyone has a house worker. If the household is not able to give an adequate wage, the house worker will live with them. Night guards are also jobs that almost everyone provides. A night guard works all night keeping watch outside your home. We heard about one Christian lady who was working 13 hours a day for only 50 cents. Her job was shelling cashew nuts.

Lunch with a Friend

Kathy and I were invited to the home of Pushpaben for lunch. As we entered the home, she was sitting on the floor cooking the meal in pots over hot coals. The next room contained two large beds, a refrigerator, and a sofa. That room was used as part kitchen, dining room, and bedroom. The food was brought in and we either sat on the bed or the floor to eat. Pushpaben was very kind to cook the food milder than they are used to. To me it was still spicy, but delicious!

Learning God's Word

Pastor Prakash is one of the few pastors I know who uses no sermon notes. I mentioned this to him, and he said he studies the passages and lets the Lord speak through him. During the Bible studies, I watched the Indian people lean forward as they listened to every word Pastor said. He beamed as he spoke of the love of Jesus. People would hang onto every word he spoke. By the end of this year, Pastor Prakash is hoping that Kathy will know the Gujarati language well enough to interpret for him for those who attend and only speak English.

Before I left for Tanzania, I entered a contest at the gym to lose weight. I did it for two reasons: one to try to get that girlish figure back; and two, to win the prize of a trip somewhere in the U.S. for my good friend and gym partner, Margaret. After packing for Tanzania, I discovered a third reason for my weight loss. Since I had the keyboard and my other luggage consisting of items for the missionaries and gifts for the Indian ladies, I had no room for my clothes. For the first time I was able to wear Kathy's clothes—perfect timing. Incidentally, I did win the contest, losing 22 lbs. Actually, there were two of us—me, the 60-year-old determined lady, and a man in his early thirties who also lost 22 lbs. (his original weight was 355 lbs.).

Egypt

Kathy and I went on a short trip to Egypt since it is not far from Tanzania. There we celebrated her birthday. We had a wonderful time visiting pyramids, temples, museums, and the Nile. In Kathy's words, "It was awesome". By the way, our guide asked the question which is asked of all tourists—does a pyramid have three sides or four sides? Answer: four sides.

Happy Birthday, Kathy!

Our Egyptian travel guide spoke very broken English. With Kathy's experience with Swahili and the Indian Gujarati languages, she was better able to understand him than I was. She often became my interpreter for our guide. One day when I was alone with our guide, he asked me about "Eternity", or at least I thought that is what he said. I was SO EXCITED he asked me that I immediately explained to him what the Bible has to say about heaven and eternity. When I finished, he had a very puzzled look on his face, ruffled through his paperwork, and pointed to the word "Itinerary". Whoops—he got a Bible lesson that he really wasn't asking for. The Lord works in mysterious ways.

Amazing Egypt

Looking Back

For those of you who receive Kathy's quarterly letters in the mail, you will recall the January 2004 letter with a picture of Kathy, five other women, and two children. A friend of mine pointed out that all are beaming with beautiful smiles and yet the two women who do not know our Lord were without smiles, looking sad and serious. (If anyone is interested in receiving Kathy's letters telling of her missionary work in Tanzania, please let me know.)

Home Again

After being gone for nearly the entire month of January, Kathy and I said some tearful good-byes at the airport, and I was off for those long flights home. Upon arriving at the San Francisco Airport, my dear friend, Esther, was waiting for me with a beautiful bouquet of flowers. We had a pleasant drive back to Sacramento, and as she was leaving she handed me a bag of groceries, knowing I would have an empty refrigerator and be too tired to go to the store!

It was so good to come home and see Shawn, Liz, Derrick, and baby Jonathan, Our family is so blessed with many friends and relatives who have supported us, prayed for us, and shown love to us over the years. I thank you all.

Jonathan and Derrick. Gifts from God.

With much love,

Carol Keller

John 15:17 ". . . love one another."

Best Team Ever!

Reflections on my mission trip to Tanzania

Tanzania – July 20 – August 20, 2012
Written for my church newsletter

After 30 hours of travel, I arrived safely in Dar es Salaam, Tanzania, East Africa, at 3 AM on July 21. On Monday my daughter, Kathy, and I with a few of her team members went to a beach about an hour away from Kathy's house to spend the week--their first vacation. It was very touching for me to see that this group (2 couples and 2 single women) worked together for six months, and yet they were excited about spending their vacation together. I asked the team for suggestions on the title of my reflections, and one of the men immediately said, "Best Team Ever!"

Kathy and I then went to Zambia and Zimbabwe to see Victoria Falls (one of the Seven Wonders of the World), which has been a dream of mine for quite some time. The sites were amazing! Each day we visited the Falls, there was a beautiful huge rainbow with colors so brilliant. It was neat to see the rainbow and remember God's promise never again to flood the earth. From there we visited Cape Town in South Africa, which is a beautiful city near where the Atlantic and Indian Oceans meet. While traveling we were able to dine on both crocodile and ostrich!

For the last two weeks of my trip, I returned to Dar es Salaam to work with Kathy and her team of Global workers. We have been preparing for a Gospel Friday Night Club, which is quite similar to AWANA in the States except they use chronological Bible storying from Genesis to Revelation through the entire Bible to share the message of redemption through Jesus Christ. I was also able to visit two of the schools that she works with and hear them dialogue about upcoming partnerships. It has been fun to see Kathy and her team learning the mother tongue of the people she works with: Gujarati. It is a tough assignment for them, but they are all giving it their best daily, meeting with language helpers and walking the streets of the city practicing what they learn.

It has been interesting to experience Ramadan while living with Kathy in her city. Kathy's room overlooks a beautiful Mosque, and it has been quite an experience learning more about their culture. For one month they do not eat or drink anything during daylight hours and observe special times of prayer. I have also learned a little bit about trying to respect their culture by dressing conservatively and being careful not to eat or drink in public during Ramadan. These are a beautiful people that we love and want to share our lives and God's grace with through our words and actions.

I have watched Kathy in her new leadership role leading a team of new Global workers. She is an excellent leader, and I don't say that just because

I am her mom, others here have made similar comments. I am excited to see new workers trained for God's glory. I pray that each one of them will continue to grow in their language and culture learning, and ultimately their love for God's creation and desire to see reconciliation made between God and man.

This is a wonderful experience being here. I wish you all could see the sights and hear the sounds of Dar es Salaam. It is truly a life-changing experience.

Now for the rest of the story . . .

A Smile is a Gift

On my return flight home, the airplane was to leave Dar es Salaam at 3:00 AM but was delayed and didn't leave until 5:00 AM. I arrived in Istanbul, Turkey—2 hours late. As I got in the long line to get my boarding pass--trying to persuade security to let me in front of the line without success—I finally got the pass but had to get in another long line for passport control/baggage. I ran as fast as I could to the gate and when arriving found only employees there. I tried to ask someone if I missed the flight; no one would say anything. Realizing the plane was gone; I asked firmly "What do I do now?" I was told to go back to the line where I received my boarding pass to get the next flight out which would be the next morning.

As the employee at the counter was filling out paperwork, I noticed she was charging me for the flight. I explained *their* flight was two hours late! She removed the charge. For three hours I stood at the counter as streams of people received their boarding passes, new tickets, etc. Feeling a little nervous about being alone and half way across the world from home, I decided not to go there in my thinking and thanked God He was with me every step of the way.

Finally, an employee approached me with my new ticket. Wondering if I would have to sleep in the airport or outside the airport, I was happy to learn I would be put up in a hotel and given meal tickets. My next long line was to go through passport control to get into Turkey. As the agent looked at my passport, he said I did not have a visa for Turkey. My heart sank as he pointed and said go over to that office and get a visa. Another line! The good news is that the visa was only $12 where in Tanzania the visa is $100. Thankfully I had a few dollars with me.

O.K., back to the long line at passport control. By then I could feel tears ready to flow. At that very moment, a small, elderly man in front of me turned around with the most beautiful smile on his face. I said, "Thank you for that smile." He replied, "You needed a smile?" I said "very badly." He turned around again and said, "A smile is a gift." At that moment, everything that happened in the past 24 hours was all worth it. Now I think of a smile as a gift!

Let's all give that gift every time we see someone.

JAPAN

My roommate from many years ago wrote and asked if I would come to Japan -- with her. The trip would consist of a tour guide named Yoko, and 16 people from all over the U.S. It would include three nights in Tokyo; 13 nights visiting cities including Hakone, Kanazawa, and Kyoto; and three nights in Hiroshima. Never having been to Japan it sounded exciting, so I said yes.

The Number 4

What I am about to write now may seem very strange to you, but I will write it anyway. As long as I can remember, the number 4 has always been my favorite number. After being married, I didn't feel our family was complete until there were four of us. Over the years, when I have felt discouraged and in need of reassurance, the Lord has used this number to remind me He is with me in everything I do.

A couple of weeks before leaving for Japan, everything seemed to be going wrong—my car breaking down, discovering mold in my home, and other matters coming up that needed to be taken care of right away. Then there was my health. I was very lethargic, problems with my throat, congestion, sinuses, and arthritis. It was one of those times in our lives when we are not sure we are going to make it through another day. I was beginning to have doubts that I should be going on this trip—and if, in fact, the trip was actually going to happen. My friend who offered to take care of both Molly and Sadie (the pups) told me I was acting so stressed that she didn't want to answer her phone when I called because I was stressing her out.

Since my flight out of San Francisco Airport was early morning, August 4, I decided to stay at a motel near the airport the night before and take a shuttle in the morning. My friend drove me to the motel and that is when the Lord began letting me know He was with me, and all would be well. At the check-in counter, I was given the key to my room—No. 144. After calling for a 6 o'clock wake-up call, I fell asleep. I woke in the middle of the night to go to the bathroom and looked at the clock: 4:44. Then at 6:04, I awoke realizing my wake-up call never came!

Checking out, I told the desk clerk I never received a wake-up call, and with much concern in his voice, he said, "I hope you didn't miss your flight". I thought to myself, "Yikes, I'm so glad I didn't. Thank you, Lord."

After a 10-hour flight, I arrived at the Narita Airport in Tokyo and took a taxi to my hotel. After a short drive, the taxi driver stopped and pointed to a 19-story building letting me know that was my hotel. Approaching the elevator, I discovered Floor 1 had a 7-Eleven Store; Floor 2 a book store; Floor 3 a business of some sort; and there it was—Floor 4 Hotel Reception. A peace came over me as I thought to myself, "I got your message Lord, loud and clear. You are here with me; I just need to keep my eyes on you. Thank you, thank you."

Observations

The population of Japan is about 127 million. Japan is an extremely clean country. There is no garbage on the streets and no cans to put garbage in. Yoko often reminded us to hang on to our garbage until we got back to our hotel.

I now know why the Japanese women have beautiful, silky skin—they never let the sun touch their skin. Nearly everyone wears a hat or carries an umbrella. When trying to guess the age of Japanese women, we usually guessed several years younger than they actually were. When going outside, Yoko would wear a hat and cover her arms with long black gloves. When trying to locate her, I would look for the lady with the black arms.

Rather than shake hands, hug, or kiss, everyone bows. It is a sign of respect, and I might add, a good way to stay healthy. When on a train, it was interesting to note that whenever a member of the train crew walked through a car, before leaving through the door, he/she would turn and bow. When making a purchase in a store, a tray is given to you to put your money on and the change is returned in the tray. No need to touch hands.

One of the most surprising things is that hardly anyone spoke English. We used a lot of sign language everywhere we went—the restaurants, stores, even the hotel employees. I asked Yoko why people don't speak English and she replied, "Why? We don't need English." My roommate and I wondered if many Japanese have the ability to speak English, but just prefer not to. One example would be when I was purchasing a donut. A handsome young man was trying to communicate with me speaking Japanese and we were not getting anywhere. I said to my roommate, "He's a cutie!" When he heard that, he had the biggest grin on his face! Yoko told us at 9 PM we could get the news on TV in English, "occasionally"—occasionally never happened. Every channel was in Japanese, and when we tried to watch the Olympics, they would broadcast only what the Japanese were doing. We never did discover how the U.S. was performing.

I never did see a Japanese person who was overweight. The only exception would be seeing a man who looked like he might be a Sumo wrestler.

On a workday, everyone wears a white top and black bottom. If wearing a suit, it is black and white—no brown or other color. When walking down the street, there seemed to be a sea of black and white. When a woman is asked about her job, she says she is an OL which means Office Lady. Men are promoted easier than women.

The yen is the official currency of Japan. It is easy to figure out the equivalent of the US dollar by just moving the decimal point over two places. 1,000 yen is $10 US; 10,000 yen is $100.

However, there are so many coins in all shapes and sizes that I never did figure out their value. There is no tipping waiters, taxi drivers, hotel maids, etc.

It is extremely difficult to become a citizen if you are not Japanese and born in Japan. I believe the only other nationalities you see are tourists or perhaps people from other countries on business.

When visiting a Japanese family in their home, the wife showed us her small kitchen. They are very inventive with how they use every space for storage. Built into the middle of the kitchen floor, about two feet deep, there is a large space to store pots and pans. There are two doors that cover this area, and a key is used to raise the doors up to access the pots and pans.

We visited a Geisha entertaining house. The Geisha girls are very talented—they sing, dance, and play instruments. There ages can range from 18 to 84 years old. The 90-minute program consists of entertainment and a meal.

On buildings there are large red triangles taped to some of the windows. This tells emergency services, like firemen, which windows can be broken to enter the building.

Many Japanese had T-shirts with English lettering on them. Yoko said they usually do not know what the words mean but enjoy wearing the shirts.

After a long day of walking, my roommate and I decided to get a massage. It was located in a large department store. To our surprise, massages are given with all your clothes on. It was very relaxing, but seemed odd to be totally dressed, lying behind a thin curtain in a department store.

One evening we went to a park next to our hotel. We were amazed to see probably a hundred people all staring at their cell phones walking around. They were all playing Pokemon Go. Some of the museums we visited would have a sign saying, "No Pokemon Go". It amazed me to see small children walking around while their parents were glued to Pokemon Go. I kept my eye on a little girl who had lost sight of her parents and was frantically searching for them. She finally found them—glued to their Pokemon Go. I thought to myself, there is no way we would let children here be free to roam in a crowded park.

Most every day was very hot and humid. Open markets would have huge chunks of ice outside for folks to come by and touch the ice to cool off. I gave one a big hug. Japan, in August, is like being in a sauna most every day. The temperatures ranged in the high 80's and 90's with 95% humidity.

Many people have some very unusual looking dogs. Most of the dogs wear some type of outfit. One dog was dressed in a shirt, plaid pants, a hat and glasses.

Early one morning we went bird watching. Two bird watching volunteers would listen for the sound of a bird and when unable to see it they would whip out a booklet showing us a picture of the appropriate bird. However, we never did see a bird, but heard several.

Food and Drinks

Of course, their main foods are rice and sushi. Not as common are whale meat, sparrow, and quail. At one of the world's largest fish markets, we saw thin rods placed through the bodies of the fish to keep them fresh. At our buffet breakfast I chose what I thought was a hardboiled egg. After cracking the egg, I discovered the yolk was hard cooked and the white was runny. Never could figure out how they did that. I was told this kind of egg is eaten over white rice.

Fruit is very expensive in Japan. If served in a restaurant there were usually only a couple pieces of pineapple or watermelon. One day I was craving some fruit and found yummy looking huge green grapes. I purchased a package of about two handfuls. It cost me $8.00! Yoko said a watermelon can range from $100 to $300 each. The one thing 1 will say is the fruit that they do have in the market is delicious and huge—apples, and peaches are the size of small melons. It can cost $13 for one large rock oyster, $10 for a few bananas, and $100-150 for one large crab. When purchasing a sandwich, the crust is removed from all white bread sandwiches—brown bread crust stays on.

Tea and Sake are favorite drinks. When visiting a Sake Museum we were shown the seven steps to making Sake. There were vending machines that you could purchase Sake drinks, Sake candy and cookies, and Sake cosmetics. Since anyone can make a purchase with a machine, I asked Yoko if children can buy Sake cookies and Sake candy. She replied, "Children can buy anything".

Going to a store was a challenge—everything was in Japanese. Sometimes there would be pictures on boxes, but no English describing the contents. On one occasion I found English. I purchased a bag with a picture of potato chips on it. The only English on the bag read: "This food is made from carefully selected ingredients and methods. Hope this food will bring you a wonderful time."

We saw a demonstration of how they make gold leaf—a very, very thin gold paper. I had mentioned that I purchased some gold leaf on a trip to China, and it is so frail I didn't know what to do with it. Yoko said, "Eat it!" It was then that I realized the gold flakes that the stores sprinkle on ice cream is paper!

Hotels

Staying two nights in a hotel in the mountains and seeing Mount Fuji was a great experience. There were individual bathhouses to soak in mineral water. Also, there were separate public bathhouses for men and for women. They were large rooms with many showers and a pool. I wondered how many tourists were brave enough to shower in the same room with strangers. Our shower experience was at a time when traffic was at a "bare" minimum.

On the bed was a Yukata Kimono—a long robe that could be worn to breakfast or to the public or private baths. There were directions as to how to put it on, and what not to do. "Do not put the right side of the Yukata over the left side—this is the way Japanese people dress corpses."

One hotel had a special room for smoking—about 5' x 8'. It was so smoky you could hardly see the people inside. It appeared you didn't have to bring your own cigarettes, just inhale.

The Toilet

I never thought I would have so much to say about a toilet as I do now! It was a little surprising the first couple times to sit down and a warm cushion type seat awaited you.

One almost needs a manual to use the toilet. There is a panel of buttons attached to the toilet which you push for the desired effect: Spray, Bidet, water pressure, standby, stop, warm, warmer, a music symbol, etc., etc. The choices!
One stall had a container on the wall with some kind of solution requesting that you clean the toilet seat before leaving.

When opening the stall door to another toilet, the lid automatically rises. After use, the lid automatically closes and flushes.

The stall doors are often labeled "Western" and "Eastern". You can choose between sitting comfortably or squatting comfortably.

On the trains, the signs on the bathroom doors were: one door a picture of a man, and the other door a picture of a man and woman. Interesting.

Transportation

Transportation is pretty amazing, modern and highly developed. There are buses, taxicabs, streetcars, subways, trains, and the famous Bullet train. The Bullet train travels 200 miles an hour—the smoothest train ride I have ever been on. The Bullet train will travel 3 hours for $150 while a regular train travels the same distance in 20 hours for $60.

On one of our train rides, after traveling an hour, the train stopped to change directions and we then turned our seats around so that we would be facing forward.

We passed a train that had orange box cars with huge letters "Women Only". Those particular cars get so crowded that they do not allow men and women to ride together.

The taxi drivers wear white gloves, a hat, and have white lace covering the top of the seats. Since they drive on the left side of the street, when a taxi pulls up, the back-passenger door automatically opens. You seldom get in a taxi on the right side. When everyone is in, the door automatically closes. One taxi driver had a small television next to his steering wheel. He was pointing to the Olympics for us to see. I must say it was a little scary to watch him drive and watch TV!

Everywhere we went cars looked like they were brand new having just gone through a car wash with a wax job. I have never seen so many new looking cars, and I can recall only seeing one with a dent. They have an interesting license plate system: yellow plates are for small cars (they can receive discounts), white plates are for large cars and trucks, and green plates are for taxicabs.

At one gas station, the nozzles to the gas pumps hung above the cars. The gas station attendant would pull the nozzle down, fill the tank, and wash the car's windows. Remember the olden days when we had that kind of service?

Religions in Japan

Our tour guide told us there were 70% Buddhists, 50% Shinto, and 1% Christian. When we mentioned that didn't calculate to 100, she said many Japanese are both Buddhists and Shinto. We visited a Japanese family and as the husband was showing us his home with his Buddhist and Shinto items of worship, he said he is both Buddhist and Shinto and one day a year—December 25, Christmas—he is a Christian!

There are thousands of Buddhist Temples and Shinto Shrines throughout Japan. In Kyoto, alone, there are 1,700 Buddhist Temples and 300 Shinto Shrines.

Buddhism

When praying to Buddha, the right hand is a little higher than the left hand (left is self, right is Buddha).

Buddhist 5 commandments:

1. Do not kill
2. Do not steal
3. Do not indulge in sexual misconduct
4. Do not make false speech
5. Do not take intoxicants

Yoko told us in Zen Buddhism, three things never change:

1. Everything will change.
2. We don't exist
3. You believe the first two; you become happy and can go to Nirvana.

One of the Buddhist Temples we visited has a statue of a doctor outside the temple. Legend says he was kicked out of the temple by Buddha because he talked too much. Yoko told me to touch the statue and then touch my knee—my arthritis will be healed. I am still waiting for the healing.

In a Buddhist cemetery, if a family cannot afford a family plot, they place ashes in what they call the "hotel" gravesite.

Hanging on the outside of one storefront are stuffed animals in the shape of "monkeys" that supposedly take away sins and evil spirits.

Daimonji is a festival of five giant bonfires lit each year on mountains in Kyoto. It signifies the moment when the spirits of deceased family members, who are said to visit this world, are believed to be returning to the spirit world.

Shinto

When approaching a Shinto Shrine, you bow twice, clap your hands twice to get the god's attention (to really make sure he hears you, you ring a loud bell), and then you make a wish.

Visiting one Shinto Shrine there are many protected roaming deer. Looking for food, they can become aggressive so we were told to show our hands empty and they will walk away. Their horns are cut off so they won't fight each other. Food for the deer can be purchased. It was fun having them eat right out of your hand.

Witnessing—Seeds Planted

Whenever I travel, the first thing I do when entering my hotel room is check all the drawers to see if there is a Bible (distributed by Gideons International). If there is, I place it on the table stand. Not one of our hotels in Japan had a Bible. In one hotel I discovered there was a book on Buddhism.

I would approach the hotel desk with a map of the city asking to please show me where there is a church. The clerk would circle a Buddhist Temple. I would show my cross neckless and say, "A Christian church". Once they circled a Catholic Church located on the outskirts of the city. Otherwise, they found no other churches.

Whenever I saw a lady wearing a cross necklace, I would comment on how pretty it was and ask if she were a Christian. Every response was no. I never did find a Christian. The more time I spent in a place where I could not find Christians, the more I realized how wonderful it is to live where we are surrounded by our Christian friends and family, knowing they were just a phone call away for support and fellowship.

When I asked Yoko what her religion was, she said she was confused. She has had teaching in Buddhism, Shinto, and a little Christianity. As soon as she said that, I immediately shot up a prayer that the Lord would prepare her heart and my heart for her to hear the Gospel. Because of our extremely busy schedule, I prayed for a time I could speak to her alone. That time did come, and I shared the Gospel with Yoko. A seed planted.

One evening, I couldn't sleep. So that I would not wake up my roommate, I went into the bathroom and prayed and read my Bible. I felt I should write down the countries and purpose for mission trips I had been on. The next day, at lunch, I sat with a lady from our group. She asked me about my mission trips. Word had gotten around I was a Christian and went on mission trips. I was prepared and witnessed to her. A seed planted.

One other opportunity arose to share my faith was when I had lunch with one of the couples from our group. They asked me about Kathy's ministry and my mission trips. A seed planted.
Before leaving Japan, I wrote a thank you to our tour guide, Yoko, and shared the love of Jesus telling her I would pray for her daily that she, too, would know the love and peace of Jesus. Yoko spoke so much about wanting peace.

Meeting with the Lord on Sunday

Nagasaki Peace Park is a park located in Nagasaki, Japan, commemorating the atomic bombing of the city on August 9, 1945 during World War II. It is next to the Atomic Bomb Museum and near the Peace Memorial Hall.

It was Sunday and learning that a Christian man created the Peace Park, I was determined to "go to church" so I decided to meet the Lord there. It was a wonderful time walking through the gardens, praying, looking at all the different monuments, and just thanking the Lord for all His blessings. I always carry a New Testament with me, so I decided to randomly open it and read the first verse I saw. It read, "What is the source of quarrels and conflicts among you? Is not the source your pleasures that wage war in your members?" (NASB) I thought, how appropriate, being where I was. I slipped a piece of paper to hold the spot in my New Testament to read it again later.

Homeward Bound

The night before we were to leave to go home, I talked with my roommate telling her about my "favorite number 4". Thank you again, Lord! I also told her I "went to church" at the Peace Park spending time with the Lord. I opened my New Testament to read her the verse and with a surprise I saw that the verse was James chapter 4 verse 1. Thank you, Lord, —another reminder that You are always there for me.

Sayonara Japan

Footnote: Arriving at the San Francisco Airport I proceeded to U.S. Customs and Border Protection screening. I noticed a new system had been set up to expedite the entry of passengers back into the States. There are over 30 machines to check out (much like the small check-out machines in a grocery store). There are large numbers above each machine. You place your passport in a slot, press a button to have your photo taken, and a receipt comes out. That is then taken to a customs agent. As my turn came to be told which machine to go to, I was told—you guessed it-- Number 4.

Paris via Uber

When we focus on the Lord, it always amazes me who and what He brings into our lives.

First a visit to BIOLA

My grandson, Derrick, attends BIOLA University (Bible Institute of Los Angeles). On April 7, 2017, I flew to LAX to attend Grandparents Day. It was so much fun touring the University and hanging out with Derrick. On April 9, I then flew to Paris to be with Kathy.

Watch out Uber drivers, here I come!

I was so excited that I had learned how to use Uber with my cell phone! With each driver, I sat in the front seat so I could have a captive audience to share Jesus.

My first experience was going from LAX to a motel near BIOLA. Gennady was the Uber driver. He is a Jew and originally from Russia. He told me because of discrimination against the Jews, his dream was to come to a free country—America. We had a great time talking and laughing. As I began sharing the Gospel, I realized that there is a tendency for people to get us off course. He talked about how he was so upset that churches, pastors, priests, are always asking for money. I asked him if he believes in the Old Testament, and he said yes. I made reference to the many times God told the people to give a tenth of their first crops. We had a wonderful conversation, and as I was getting out of the car, I told him I always feel it is an honor to meet one of God's chosen people, and that I would pray for him. I told him he would make a wonderful Christian!

The next Uber driver was Martin. As we began talking, he said he has a relative who is so frightened because she says we are in the last days. He asked if I feel the same, and I told him the Bible says no one knows the day or the time, so I am not concerned. Martin mentioned that he recently quit smoking. I was so excited for him that as I left, I said I would pray for him. He said, "Will you pray for my two-year-old daughter, too?" I said, of course, I would be happy to.

Cristian was my third driver. I said all you need is an "h" in your name and it would be Christian. I asked if he was a Christian. Because of his reaction, I felt the Lord telling me to back off. I didn't want to scare him away and leave him with a negative impression of the Lord. I try to be very sensitive and share only what I feel the Lord wants me to share.

More about my God appointed experiences later.

Off to Paris

On April 8, I stayed at a motel near the Los Angeles Airport so I could catch my early flight on Sunday. Kathy sent me a last-minute text. She asked if it would be possible for me to bring some A-1 Sauce. You cannot buy it in Paris, and she wanted to share it with her French friends. I didn't think it would be possible because there was no grocery store anywhere near the motel. Adjacent to the motel was a Denny's Restaurant where I went for dinner. As I looked around at the tables, there it was—A-1 Sauce! I got the bright idea to ask if I could purchase a bottle, so I explained my predicament to the restaurant manager, and he was happy to sell me a bottle of A-1 Sauce--yea for Denny's.

Arriving in Paris, I discovered that Paris was on high alert especially at the airport. There were uniformed security guards, policemen, and military carrying machine guns—the closest I have ever come to such a huge gun.

The first alert was due to Holy Week (Easter). Upon approaching a church, at the entrance would be a sign stating, "Enter at your own risk. You could be searched and questioned at any time".

The second week I was there high alert was due to the presidential election. There were 10 candidates, nine men and one woman. On that weekend, one man and the woman were voted to run in the final election. Kathy received an email message from the Evangelical Free Church Mission French leader. He wrote that a French government official contacted him stating that all missionaries should be warned not to go near any tourist attractions during the election. The most we did during the election weekend was ride the train. That in itself was a little scary with hundreds of passengers coming and going—the perfect target. There were military and police on duty at every train station.

Kathy commented that twice a week, Jewish children go to a synagogue during the day, and military are posted outside to protect the children.

The French people reminded me of a mission trip I went on in Russia. If people do not know you, they do not speak or smile when you look at them. Russian people do the very same thing. I thought about my friend and neighbor Margaret who would have a difficult time in France. When we take walks together, she greets everyone who comes in earshot of her with a big smile and a how are you today. However, in France when you do know someone, you get a kiss on each cheek. It was fun seeing men comfortably acknowledging each other in this way.

The food was delicious. I have never eaten so much bread, cheese, and pastry. I know it was the Lord's perfect timing for me to go to Paris. A few weeks before leaving, I was under so much stress that I lost 12 pounds. After eating the amazing food in Paris, I gained back 10 pounds! Did I mention bread, cheese, and pastry? By the way, I am sorry to say our pastry doesn't compare to the yummy pastry in France. However, one food I could not eat was Steak Tartare—raw beef!

Their transportation system is amazing. Upon entering a train station, you hardly ever wait more than five or 10 minutes for your train. And talk about people--hundreds coming and going all day long. When traveling during work hours in the morning, all you hear is the sound of the train. No one speaks. In the afternoon on the way home from work, acquaintances talk with each other-- guess they are happy the work day is over.

Kathy, the French language, and Ministry

Besides learning all about the French culture, unreached places and people in Paris, Kathy wants to fluently speak the French language right now! It was a good experience that I was there because she had many opportunities to practice interpreting French to English and vice versa. Having learned the Swahili and Gujarati languages, she thought French would be somewhere in the middle. However, she discovered French is a very difficult language to learn.

I was told that the French language has lots of puckering; therefore, a woman will end up with lots of wrinkles under her nose.

I love being Kathy's full-time secretary, and she definitely put me to work on this visit. With focusing on learning the French language, starting new ministries, and all the paperwork/computer work she has to do, she really does need a secretary. Anyone out there want to volunteer?

She is beginning to recruit her team. We had

lunch with a very sweet lady, a fellow student in Kathy's language school. Lisa recently retired, from her coaching job in Texas. She loves Paris and wants to live there and do missionary work. She may become Kathy's first team member. Please let Kathy know if you know of anyone interested in missionary work in Paris.

Kathy is getting involved in a ministry to homeless women. Also, the established Muslim community is working with her church to reach out to Muslim women and children who are homeless. It is a wonderful opportunity to share the Gospel with the Muslim community.

She had prayed about a ministry with youth in the church she is now attending. When we attended Easter Sunday church service, the children were excused to go to Sunday school. A young woman approached Kathy and asked if she would help out in the Junior High class. She was so excited! God answered her prayer. He often answers prayers in such fun and unexpected ways!

She recently discovered that many French people enjoy Black Gospel music. Her Church is forming a group to sing the music in French and English. Kathy will be singing, probably in both languages.

The lady she rents her room from, Francoise, is a wonderful lady. She says Kathy is her second daughter. I have met many of Francoise's friends. Please pray as Kathy shares with them that someday they will become Christians.

Homeward bound

Kathy put me on the train to the airport. French people are very kind and helpful. I had help with my luggage on the escalator. A man helped me with my luggage as I struggled to get through the swinging door leaving the train station. At one of the trains stops, I noticed six men and women enter the train—they were dressed in red and black uniforms and I thought, how nice, they must be from the Salvation Army. To my surprise, they were train employees checking to see if all the passengers had tickets. They wrote out tickets to a couple passengers—not the kind of tickets they really wanted to receive.

Upon arriving in LAX, I went to South West Airlines to see if I could get an earlier flight to Sacramento. As I approached the airline employee, 1 did my usual thing by finding something I could say that is positive about the person I am speaking with. With his dark skin and light blue eyes, I told him he had beautiful eyes. He arranged for me to get a flight within the hour. He asked, "Do you know why you got an earlier flight? Because you were so kind."

I raced to the luggage check point which was having serious backup problems. A man motioned for me to come forward. He asked me my age. When I told him, he asked if I have any metal implants. Stating I did not, he waved me on ahead of everyone else. I told him, "I guess it pays to be old!"

On the flight to Sacramento, the seat in front of me was occupied by a Hindu man who sat next to an elderly lady. He began talking to her about the Hindu religion concerning heaven and hell. I leaned forward to hear what he had to say. He said if you don't have God, then you are in hell right now. He asked the lady if she believed in God. She began witnessing to him about God, Jesus, and the Bible. He commented, "You really do know Him. You are glowing." She gave him her phone number and said, "Pray to Jesus, and when you find Him, call me." I thought to myself, wouldn't it be wonderful if people would see us "glowing" as we spoke of Jesus! After the plane landed, I spoke with the lady. Her name is Ann Maxine Nivens and she told me she wrote a book entitled *Sweet Summer.* I am looking forward to reading it.

Arriving at the Sacramento Airport, I called, yes, you guessed it, Uber for a ride home. Because Paris is nine hours ahead of us, my body felt like it was 3 o'clock in the morning. As I got into the car, I learned that the driver, Sulaiman, was from Afghanistan. I thought to myself, "Oh Lord, I am so tired! Do you really want me to talk to this young man?" After mentioning I am a Christian, he excitedly told me his family is Christian, and that he just finished reading the Bible all the way through. It took him 90 days. Sulaiman attends American River College. It was wonderful just listening to him and hearing the excitement in his voice of what the Lord is doing in his life. I was so happy to just listen to him. I asked him if he enjoyed being an Uber driver. He said, "Yes because I can meet people like you". I told him, "And I can meet people like you".

Now that I have returned home, I can't wait to see what the Lord has for me next!

Footnotes:

Kathy ordered flowers to be sent to me for Mother's Day. I didn't receive them, and after contacting the company she realized she ordered the flowers in French—Mother's Day in France is May 26! I received beautiful flowers on France's Mother's Day.

She also gave me a 3,000-piece puzzle (47"x33")! It is a picture of an open-air market entitled "La Vucciria Market, Palermo". The largest puzzles I have put together have been 1,000 pieces. Better go get started!

About the Author

Carol Keller lives in Sacramento, California. She has two children Kathy and Shawn, and three grandchildren Derrick, Jonathan, and Kaleigh.

She is thankful to the friends who encouraged her to write this book.

She is especially thankful to Tyler, for all the hours he spent "helping a friend" understand all the computer and technical stuff, and to Maxine, for reading over the first draft of her book and performing the first round of editing.

Most of all she is thankful to the Lord for the amazing experiences and opportunities He has given her to share His love in many parts of the world.

41640671R00051

Made in the USA
Middletown, DE
09 April 2019